Mind Your Own Business

by

Dr. Erin Oksol

ISBN: 978-1-5136-4373-1

Published by Heather Andrews:
http://followitthrupublishing.com/

Cover by Lorraine Shulba: www.bluebugstudios.com

Edited by Patty Lauterjung

Copy Edited by Amanda Horan: www.letsgetbooked.com

Proofread by Suzanne LaVoie: www.suzannelavoiewrites.com

Formatted by Bojan Kratofil: www.expertformatting.com

This book is dedicated to my husband, Garth.

Thank you for your *unstoppable love* for me.

Thank you for your *unstoppable belief* in me.

Thank you for your *unstoppable support* of me.

Thank you for your *unstoppable leadership* in
our family.

Thank you for your *unstoppable loyalty* to being
your best.

Because of you, *I am unstoppable.*

Table of Contents

Foreword

Before you begin *Mind Your Own Business*, please take a moment and congratulate yourself. You've taken the first key step in transforming your mind and growing your business to new and exciting levels.

How do I know this book can significantly change your life? Because I've watched my wife, Dr. Erin, use these same tools to do exactly that. Less than three years ago, in 2016, she had a vision and a desire to change. She was always very good at helping people change their mindset; after all, she had a successful private practice in psychology for sixteen years. However, the work became tedious. She was forced to work more as her hourly rate decreased year after year due to changes in the health insurance industry. Erin realized this was not sustainable, but knew she was made for greatness and could do more.

My wife loves consuming information and using it to help people. She has always been a champion of improving herself. Erin was on a mission. "What vehicle could allow me to use my skills most effectively and at the same time help others improve themselves?" she asked herself. It was at that time that Erin discovered business coaching. It was a perfect fit. My wife has the training, experience, knowledge, and vision to help people become unstuck, realize their potential, and reach higher levels of success.

When Erin and I first looked at the business coaching industry, we saw a lot of people who were, in my opinion, *cliché coaches*. "If you visualize it, it will become a reality." "Work smarter, not harder." "If you can believe it, you can achieve it." While there is truth to these statements, the vast majority of coaches I saw did not have any substance behind their statements.

My wife is different. She understands the science behind these statements, can interpret them for you, and teach you how to implement them strategically into your life to create real and meaningful results.

What truly sets Erin apart from the masses of other business coaches is not just her doctorate in psychology (although that's a big one), or her mini-library of business and self-help books she has consumed in the last twenty-seven months (I think her Amazon account has a full-time employee). My beautiful and brilliant wife has an innate ability to love others and truly want them to succeed. It amazes me how genuinely excited she gets when a client discovers growth in their business. She leads with her generous heart and instructs with her amazing mind. It's never about her; it's always about *you*. Her humility is something to behold.

You may think I am biased (which I am), but I see how others respond to my wife. They are blown away by her intelligence and her ability to see in others what they don't see in themselves. One of the many things I fell in love with is how she wears her emotions on her sleeve. Some may view this as a weakness, but it is undeniably an incredible strength. People are drawn to the passion she exudes. She loves to laugh, and people love to laugh with her; you will find a lot of humor in this book.

Erin is the biggest cheerleader I know and is constantly cheering (loudly) for others from the sidelines. Everything about working with my wife is fun, yet laser-focused on getting you to the level of success you have desired.

Now about this book…

I've seen the fear and trepidation of writing her first solo book (she's human, after all). My wife's strength is how she recognizes and then overcomes fear. She began and set off on a firestorm of writing, completing multiple chapters a day. How did she write so fast? Because everything Erin has done for the past twenty years in her career and life has led up to this moment in time. This book. These skills she wants you to learn. These twenty-one days of change.

Think about that for a minute. In twenty-one short days, you will have the tools you need to up-level your business, success, and happiness. Years of information absorbed and interpreted by my wife, right at your fingertips. I'm an engineer and understand the importance of having the best tools close by, at the right time. *Mind Your Own Business* is a quick and easy daily read that lays out the roadmap for your success, and the right time to get started is now.

I cannot wait to see and hear how high you go and how many obstacles you successfully overcome along the way. I know my wife will want to know about them too!

I wish for you all the things you wish for yourself. Now turn the page and let the excitement begin!

Garth Oksol,
Dr. Erin's husband and biggest fan.

Acknowledgments

I didn't learn to mind my own business alone. This book is truly the culmination of years of education, mentorship, and friendship from so many.

First, thank you God for my life. Thank you for your grace and the calling you have placed over my life. Thank you for your constant downloads of ideas and visions for my life and my work and for guiding me to best serve your people. All that I do, I do to glorify you.

Thank you to my husband Garth. Thank you for supporting every single thing I want to do. Thank you for cooking, cleaning and taking care of our children when I need to be taking care of others, myself, and our vision. You make me look insanely productive and help me be insanely happy. You say you are my biggest fan and I am yours.

Thank you to my children, Grace, Emily, and Zachary for your belief in me, your encouragement of me, and your excitement for me. I love sharing the good, the bad, and the ugly with you. I love that we are a team. My wins are your wins.

Thank you to the mentors, educators, and influencers who have significantly impacted my life and my work. Thank you for stepping into your greatness. It gave me permission to step into mine. These giants include: Brendon Burchard, Oprah Winfrey, Marianne Williamson, John Piper, Gabby Bernstein, Dr. Steven Hayes, Grant Cardone, Dr. William O'Donohue, Seth Godin and Marie Forleo.

Thank you to the following coaches and consultants who significantly helped me grow my business and my mindset: Jonathan Manske, Kevin Ciccotti, Jennifer Darling, Jonathan

Perez, Elizabeth Bachman, Caterina Rando, Jay Fiset, Jessica Caver Lindholm, Marcia O'Malley, Alexanne Stone, Anna Gaspari, and Brynn Breuner.

In life and business, we need people to champion for us. I am so grateful for my friends and colleagues who have advocated for me, referred to me, and believed in me. Thank you Desiree Chapman, Laura Watson, Nicole Howell, Johnny Lujan, Ly Smith, Pamela Zimmer, the members and board of Professional Saleswomen of Nevada, Jill Rutherford, Shirley Larkins, Mindy Van Vleet, Temesghen Starr, Cynthia Failor, and Wendy Lee Carrillo.

Thank you to my clients. You teach me more than I could ever teach you. Thank you for having the courage to change your life and serve more people. It has been an honor to help you rise and a joy to watch you grow.

Thank you, Debbie Patrick for helping me launch this incredible business. God knew what He was doing when He put us on adjoining lounge chairs at a small public swimming pool in Nevada. Thank you for showing me the way.

Thank you to my team member and first hire, Ann Pope. You never shy away from a challenge, you seek to make me shine, you help me serve many, and you believe in my business. Thank you for investing your heart and time into my dream. I am so grateful for you. This is just the beginning.

Thank you to my publisher and best friend, Heather Andrews. Thank you for encouraging to me to share my story years ago. Thank you for constantly leveling up so I never have to do it alone. Thank you for daily showing up in my life to laugh with me, brainstorm with me, and struggle with me. Every success is sweeter when I share it with you. I share this book with you. I know you will help so many others share their stories and gifts with the world. Thank you for helping me share mine.

And last, thank you, the reader. Thank you for aiming at greatness. Thank you for seeking excellence. Thank you for seeking significance through service to many. Thank you for reading this book and thank you in advance for what you will do with the tools you learn in these pages.

I'm AMPED for you to mind your own business,

Dr. Erin

Introduction

Welcome to your ultimate high-performance mindset manual. Twenty-one days to supercharge your success and amplify your best life. I am so glad you are here, right now, reading this book. The techniques shared here have the ability to completely transform your business and your life. Think that's a big promise? It is, and I make it because it's not magic…it's science.

There are promises behind principles. They say success leaves clues. In this book, I will give you those clues and take the guesswork out of creating sustainable success. As business owners, when we take the right actions enough times, over a long enough period of time, success is inevitable. Success cannot help but follow our lead. Our actions. Our habits. Our success thought patterns. It has nowhere else to go but up.

A Little About Me and Why it Matters to You

My name is Dr. Erin. I'm a high-performance coach, psychologist, seminar leader, four-time best-selling author, and founder of the AMPED Business Academy. For the past fifteen years, I have been *obsessed* with the psychology of success.

You will learn how to achieve lasting and extraordinary success. You will understand the formula, the science, the steps, the mindset, and the psychology behind my methods. Isn't it time to conquer your fears and be courageous enough to move to the next level and grow the successful business of your dreams?

I Understand You

You want a profitable business. You desire to help others and serve with passion. You want to make money doing what you love. You have lots of great ideas but lack a clear strategy for how to implement them. Or maybe you feel a bit overwhelmed and unsure about how to create a clear pathway to success. Perhaps you have already achieved great results, have clarity and purpose, and are ready to take your business to the next level.

I understand you because I *am* you.

Just over two years ago, in September 2016, I set out to create and launch my own profitable coaching and speaking business. I had big dreams. I wanted to be a professional speaker and host my own transformational seminars. I wanted to work with the best of the best—professional, driven, resourceful, positive, and coachable women and men who wanted to live with purpose, intention, and be greatly compensated for their work.

I knew there was greatness within me. But I struggled with knowing the exact steps to take to reach my goals. So, I hired coaches. A lot of them. I devoured books and podcasts and attended seminars and workshops to help me become a successful entrepreneur. I got busy taking massive action, building my business, my relationships, my skills, my influence, and myself.

They say your network becomes your net worth. In just one year, from 2016 to 2017, I went on 213 coffee dates. I added value wherever I could. I spoke forty-three times in front of my ideal clients that first year in business. I grew my influence on social media. I learned the psychology of sales and fell in love with selling (this psychologist never thought she would say that!).

A High-Performance Mindset is Possible for You

I promise you it's true! This mindset is available to everyone. But I want you to understand before we start…high-performance might not be what you think. It's not something that is available only for the lucky ones, or the highly-educated ones, or the ones with lots of resources. High-performance is non-discriminatory, but it requires *courage*. A lot of courage. Courage is literally the foundational building block to your success. It is the predictor of all your future success and the foundational skill that will ultimately bring joy, happiness, and confidence into your life.

And here's the best part—the aspect I love most about a high-performance mindset—it is a set of skills, so anyone can learn how to have one! This mindset is a set of tools, skills, strategies, and applied scientific research. I geek out over this stuff! And *anybody* can apply it to their business and change their life.

You know, I didn't just set out to write a book on high-performance mindset. All of this happened organically, like a natural process in life. I've been a psychologist for over fifteen years and an entrepreneur for the past eleven years, but initially, the change all started to happen because I wanted to be able to solve my pain.

Here's My Story: I'm a Lot Like You

Have you ever felt really discouraged, simply surviving in what seems a hopeless situation? Perhaps your business or life didn't turn out at all how you thought it would. No matter how hard you tried, nothing seemed to bring the success you dreamed about. Not too many years ago, I was so down and depressed, and I had so much anxiety, that I finally hit bottom and said, "Enough is enough!" I realized the pain of me staying the same was far greater than the pain of changing. I just *had* to change.

I had dreams inside that were killing me...can you relate? I wanted to be a best-selling author, but I didn't think anyone would want to hear my story. I wanted an amazing, successful business where I made great money, but I didn't have a clue how to do it effectively. I wanted to speak powerfully on stage and share my message to impact hundreds of people, but I could barely muster up the courage to speak up in business meetings. I struggled with panic attacks, which is a difficult problem.

I had all these dreams, and I wanted to succeed just once in my life. So I said, "That's it!" I rolled up my sleeves, and the scientist and the psychologist in me said, "I'm going to figure this out." They say success leaves clues, and I was out to find them.

I read stacks of books on the areas of fear, confidence, mindset, money, success, business, and speaking effectively. I listened to countless hours of podcasts to better myself and learn the business skills I needed. I interviewed experts and coaches. I went to seminars and retreats. I hired a therapist and several coaches. I was on a mission to find the recipe for success, to establish a system that I could use to solve my pain and reach the success I desired. And when I applied it to my life, everything changed in a surprisingly short amount of time.

That's When Everything Changed

I went from having no coaching business, and being limited in my psychology practice by time and money, to launching a successful coaching business—a business I am in love with, helping clients whom I love. I went from not knowing how to get published in the non-academic world to now being a four-time best-selling author. In my first year of business, I won the awards of Top 20 Most Powerful Women and Professional Saleswoman of the Year here in Nevada where I live. I went from stage fright to being a powerful keynote speaker who travels all over the country. All of that within only one year. If it didn't happen to me, I might not believe it.

I say all this not to *impress* you, but to impress *upon* you, that the plan works when you work the plan. Systems and principles have promises behind them. The key to success is understanding which principles and plans to work to ensure your own success.

And let's be clear. Without a bulletproof mindset, systems and strategies will only take you so far.

You see, when you transform your psychology, you can transform your business and life.

It's not magic…it's science. And I love sharing it with you. My joy comes from helping you achieve your big, scary, awesome goals.

My Promise to You

I have combined my experience in growing a successful business with my expertise in human psychology. This book outlines high-performance mindset strategies for entrepreneurs who want to create a profitable business while being happy, joyous, and free.

My promise to you is this. I promise if you study this book and complete the simple (but not always easy) steps that I'm going to teach here, you will create a transformation for yourself, similar to the one that I created for myself. Remember, it's not magic…it's science.

But here's the key. This is what I want you to do right now. I need for you to *commit fully*. I need you to decide to cut away any other possibility except for the one we will create together—an amped business and life. I need you to declare that it's your time to step into your greatness. It's time to be the person who says, "I'm ready. I'm willing. It's my time." Will you do that now in exchange for a future of massive success?

You won't be alone, because I'm going to be with you as your coach. In the next twenty-one days, I'm going to ask you to do things that are outside of your comfort zone. But at the end of this short amount of time, I guarantee you will experience a shift. A transformation. It's going to be an incredible journey.

Are you ready to master your mindset, increase your confidence, and own your highest power? Are you prepared to shorten your learning curve and take advantage of the proven keys to success in this remarkable and very special book? You can live the rest of your life at iconic levels of happiness, prosperity, and influence.

I cannot imagine my life without this success technology. I've helped hundreds of clients with my methods. I've seen so many people change their lives with these mindset techniques in a short amount of time. Some of the changes are immediate. It's happened in my one-to-one coaching relationships, my group coaching courses, my seminars and workshops, and in over 15,000 hours of helping people in my psychology practice. And now, I'm giving the keys to this technology to you.

I am honored to be with you these next twenty-one days. I am excited to hear how it supercharges your success. And I am thrilled for you to reap the rewards you deserve.

Ready…set…**grow**.

Day 1
Find Your
Mission

"If you don't know where you are going, you'll end up someplace else."
-Yogi Berra

Begin with the end in mind.

This insight is very true in life and in business. Let's use a car analogy. While I'm not an expert in cars, I think this really drives the point home (pun intended).

I want you to think of your business like a car. Your business is your 'vehicle' for impacting others, your vehicle for impacting your life and your family, and your vehicle for sharing your gifts and passions with the world. As business owners and entrepreneurs, we all have our own unique vehicles.

So, the first step in growing a massively successful business is figuring out where you are going. Where do you want this vehicle to take you? What is your destination?

For example, if I were to get in my car here in Nevada and want to visit Times Square in New York City, I wouldn't just hop in my car and start heading east and hope I get there. No. I would enter a very specific address into my car's navigation system and take a very specific route. The same specificity and navigation is necessary when building a massively successful business.

Your destination is simply your goal—so what do you want?

Psychologically speaking, when attempting to reach any goal, it is very important to begin with the end in mind. We know from research that the brain *loves* when we get crystal-clear on our goals. We know that what we focus on expands. As your coach, I want you to get very clear on what your ideal business looks like.

The biggest problem when we don't get specific is that we can get easily distracted. If we don't get the destination right, we can take a detour and end up in a place where we never intended to land.

It is extremely important to understand that the brain does not know when you are telling it the truth and when you are telling it a lie. It does what you tell it to do.

Let me show you right now how this works. I want you to look around and memorize everything in your surroundings that is blue. Do that for thirty seconds. Great. Now, what if I asked you, "OK, now tell me everything you just saw that was red?" Chances are you wouldn't come up with much because you were focused on the blue items.

This is how your brain will work in your business. If you concentrate on hitting an income target of $50,000, chances are you will end up closer to that target than, say $300,000. You can see that it is extremely important to get clear on a realistic, informed target.

When I hired my first coach, she asked me my income goal. I said, "I don't know…$100,000." She asked me where I came up with that number, and I had to admit I saw on social media that this somehow seemed to be the magic number where people thought they "made it." Thankfully, she had me sit down and determined my ideal budget. What kind of lifestyle did I want? How did I want to work? How often did I want to work, with whom, and doing what types of business activities? I quickly realized my income goal was much higher than I originally determined. I was able to reach for a goal that truly mattered to me, and that got me excited.

The second and extremely important exercise I want you to take to find your mission is to understand *why* you want what you want. *Why* is it so important and meaningful to you to reach your destination? The easiest way I have found to get to the heart of the issue, to your own why, is to create a simple sentence that goes like this:

"I want such and such goal so that…" Then fill in the sentence with as many reasons you can think of.

Putting the words "so that" after your stated business goals will help you discover *why* you want what you want, will motivate you, and keep you focused on reaching your destination. I like to think of your why as the fuel for your 'vehicle'. Without it, your car will break down, and your business will not succeed. Without frequent reminders of why you are doing what you are doing, you will be at risk for overwhelm, burnout, confusion, and frustration. You may also feel the urge to quit.

I always like to say that your why should make you cry. What I mean by that is your why is extremely personal, meaningful, and emotional. It should mean so much to you that it fuels you to get out of bed every day and build your dream, no matter what.

There is a wonderful saying, "When you know your *why*, you can withstand any *how*."

Dr. Erin's Call to Action

When thinking about the goals you have for your business and the destination you desire to reach, the following questions will help you achieve the laser focus that is required for success.

Ask yourself:

- What exactly will you do in your business?
- Who will benefit from your services or product?
- How much money is in your bank account?
- Where do you live?
- What kind of clothes do you wear?
- How do you spend a typical ideal day?
- Who needs to come along side you to partner with you in your business?

- What kind of personal and family relationships do you enjoy?

- How do you spend your free time?

- How many hours a week do you work?

- How do you use your money to give back and make an impact?

The answers to these questions are what you will program into your 'vehicle's' GPS system.

Day 2
Build the Muscle of Discipline

"Discipline is the bridge between goals and accomplishment."

-Jim Rohn

Go to the personal growth gym every day.

Are you ready to start flexing your muscles? No, we aren't going to the gym.

I call it the personal growth gym, and it's time to start visiting it regularly if you want massive business success. I want to share the importance of building the muscle of discipline.

This leads us to the very common, very human problem of "Why don't we do what we know we should do?" I like to call this the Knowing-Doing Gap. We've all had the painful experience of failing at a goal. We want to lose ten pounds. We know what to do—yet we don't follow through. We want to be more visible on Facebook, and we know we need to do Facebook Lives and regular posts. Yet we stay stuck, paralyzed with fear.

For years I was the queen of starting on Monday. My family would even joke that my name was Erin I-Will-Start-On-Monday Oksol. And it was funny—until it wasn't. I knew I needed discipline, and I knew I would feel so much better about myself if I had discipline.

It was my desire to live in congruence with what I stated I wanted that led me to compete in a fitness competition when I was forty-years-old. I didn't have dreams of stepping on a stage in an itsy-bitsy-teeny-weeny-turquoise-rhinestone-string-bikini. I simply wanted to stop eating cookies all the time. I wanted to stop being the woman who *said* she wanted to be healthy, but regularly ate Oreos. I wanted to be in integrity.

As a business owner, you are your own boss. While this is one of the most exciting and attractive reasons for being an entrepreneur, it also comes with some potential pitfalls and potholes. Because you don't have a boss telling you what to do and when to do it (can I get a hallelujah?), you have to be disciplined enough to keep yourself focused and on track. You have to be the one who chooses to be in integrity. You have to choose to have your behaviors match your desires and intentions. You are responsible for closing the Knowing-Doing Gap.

Being the leader of your own life requires **staying on mission.** Staying on mission is an extremely important step to creating massive business success. I am so excited to share with you my top four tips for staying committed to doing the things you said you would do, long after the motivation that was originally there leaves you. Because, believe me, it will leave. It happens to all of us. And what separates the professionals from the amateurs is your response to these distractions, doubts, fears, or stress. So, let's dive in.

Tip #1: Grow the muscle of discipline.

Here's the deal; the surest way to improve your bottom line is to improve your discipline. Think of discipline as a muscle that strengthens with use. Nobody is born with discipline; it is a learned skill. Practice makes patterns. When you practice being disciplined, you will become disciplined. And all you have to do is *decide* to become more disciplined. You are just one decision away from massive change. Isn't that exciting?

Tip #2: Hold your why so high that nothing can knock it down.

On day one you discovered your why—the deep, meaningful, extremely important reason or reasons for wanting to grow your business. Find a way to remind yourself of your why—daily. I love having people make a vision board and then asking them to look at it every single day. Change your home screen on your phone or laptop to remind you of your why. Write down your goals and read them every day. Your brain loves specificity about where it's going, and it loves to be reminded.

Tip #3: Be accountable.

Surround yourself with people who also have big dreams and goals. I call them growth friends. Find an accountability partner who you can touch base with every day, even if it's only through a text or a quick minute talking about your progress. Successful people surround themselves with other successful people. Maybe that's a mentor, a coach, a mastermind group, a business networking group, a friend, your spouse—someone who will support you on your journey as a business owner.

Tip #4: Learn how to say no. A lot.

When deciding whether you should say yes or no to something, ask yourself, "Does this contribute to or take away from my goal?" or "Does this further my mission?" I always like to remind people that when we say yes to something, we say no to something else. It's just the way it works. But most likely your no doesn't have to mean never; it may simply mean, "Not right now." There is only one of you, and your time and resources are extremely valuable. I love Oprah's take on this. She says, "You can have it all, just not on the same day."

Remember…go to the personal growth gym every day. Discipline is like a muscle. The more you use it, the stronger it will get.

Dr. Erin's Call to Action

Create your own **Not-To-Do List**.

"When you say yes to something, you say no to something else."

-Dr. Erin

List below all the things you will say no to so that you can say yes to growing your business.

____

____

____

____

____

____

____

____

____

____

____

____

____

____

____

____

____

Day 3
Slow Down
to Go *Fast*

"Assessment is today's means of modifying tomorrow's instruction."
-Carol Ann Tomlinson

In order to get to where you want to go, it is helpful first to determine where you are.

I ran a successful private practice in psychology for fifteen years. The first appointment with a new client was always about assessment. I could not possibly determine the best treatment plan for the client until I first understood the client's history, the cause of their problems, the biological and medical factors that may have contributed to their presenting issues, etc.

The same is true for your business. Before you go full-speed ahead with strategies, I want you to slow down to assess the current state of your mindset.

You might be reading this book and feel like your life and business are totally put together—you have clarity about who you are, and you're confident and optimistic that you can achieve the success you are reaching for. Or you might feel stuck, overwhelmed, scattered, full of great ideas, but lack a plan to put them all together to create that profitable business you want. Maybe you feel unsure, fearful, and even sometimes question whether you should just give up. Or maybe you're in a state of transition, figuring out your next move.

The great benefit of this assessment is that it doesn't matter where you are right now. There is always another level, and information to be gleaned by stopping to determine your current state—where you are right now in your journey.

This ten-part questionnaire is based on neuroscience research and different psychological theories including cognitive theory, behavioral theory, and goal attainment theory. In basic English, what this means is that I want to help you apply the science of success to achieve your goals as fast as possible and with as much ease and joy as possible.

I want to share with you the top ten mindset factors that will predict whether or not you will reach your goals. These ten factors will teach you what you should think about and focus on as you design your next steps to move towards that bigger vision for yourself. We know from the last thirty years of psychological research that these ten factors contribute the most to your chances of achieving success or not.

You are going to learn a lot about yourself as you complete this ten-part assessment.

Dr. Erin's Call to Action

The "How to Get Anything I Want" Assessment

Complete this strategic ten-part assessment to appraise your internal drive and motivation for success. I guarantee the answer to why you don't yet have the success you desire, and the factors that can predict your future success, are both found in this ten-part questionnaire.

Ask yourself these ten questions and give yourself a rating from 1 to 10. Honestly answer each of them, and learn how to get anything you want.

<u>Future Self/Person</u>

Can I visualize myself reaching this goal? Is this goal or activity relevant to my future identity and how I see myself spending my time in the future, over the long-term?

1   2   3   4   5   6   7   8   9   10

1 = No, not at all   10 = Yes, very much

<u>Intrinsic Motivation</u>

Is this goal or activity something I am passionate about, would enjoy doing, feel proud about, and sense contributes meaningfully? Would I do this regardless of money, status, recognition, or power (extrinsic rewards)?

1   2   3   4   5   6   7   8   9   10

1 = No, not at all   10 = Yes, very much

How's This Working for Me? (Utilitarian Value)

Is this goal or activity something that will lead to a useful outcome for me? Will I get something useful in life out of doing this?

1   2   3   4   5   6   7   8   9   10

1 = No, not at all   10 = Yes, very much

Cost/Benefit Analysis

Can I accomplish this goal while at the same time having time/energy/effort/resources and discipline needed elsewhere in my life?

1   2   3   4   5   6   7   8   9   10

1 = No, not at all   10 = Yes, very much

What's the Time Horizon?

Is this goal or activity going to have quick and recognizable results that I can enjoy soon?

1   2   3   4   5   6   7   8   9   10

1 = No, not at all   10 = Yes, very much

The "I Can Do This Factor" (Personal Control)

Is this goal or activity something that I will be able to make happen? Can I turn this goal into a reality through my efforts?

1   2   3   4   5   6   7   8   9   10

1 = No, not at all   10 = Yes, very much

Social Support

Will others support me in achieving this dream? Will others help me and cheerlead me when I attempt this?

1   2   3   4   5   6   7   8   9   10

1 = No, not at all   10 = Yes, very much

Do I Have Enough Bandwidth?

Is this goal or activity something I will have enough time and focus to do a good job?

1   2   3   4   5   6   7   8   9   10

1 = No, not at all   10 = Yes, very much

Do I Have Enough Resources?

Will I have the resources I need to successfully accomplish this goal?

1   2   3   4   5   6   7   8   9   10

1 = No, not at all   10 = Yes, very much

Personal Autonomy

Am I in control of making this goal happen? Will I have the power in decision making to achieve what I want?

1   2   3   4   5   6   7   8   9   10

1 = No, not at all   10 = Yes, very much

How to Understand and Use Your Results

If you rated yourself below a 7 on any of the questions, this is great information to have and dive deeper into.

Ask yourself:

- What would it take to increase that score to an 8 or above?

- What useful information is this score telling me?

- Why does it make perfect sense my score is this way, and how might I increase it?

- What are the pros and cons of pursuing this goal versus letting it go?

Day 4
Be **Willing** *to*
Start **Small**

"Are you willing to be embarrassed to start small?"

-Brendon Burchard

> **We all go through Suckville.**
> **Just don't stay too long.**

It was a hot 4th of July in 2016. That was the day I met Debbie. I was relaxing in a lounge chair at the local pool, sipping an ice-cold lemonade. As we sat poolside watching our children play and giggle in the water, we started chatting. After a few minutes, Debbie confidently said, "I'm a marketing guru." I shared with her the dream that was on my heart. "I want to be a speaker and impact thousands of lives. But I'm terrified and have no idea how to start."

I asked Debbie a question that I still believe to this day changed the course of my business. "I want to be a professional speaker. How the heck does one do that?" She looked at me and matter-of-factly replied, "I think you speak." After I stopped laughing, I looked at her again and asked seriously, "How does one do that?"

"That's the easy part," she said. "I'll help you with that piece."

Four coffee dates later, we had mapped out my brand, message, and signature speech. Debbie also helped me book my first speaking gig. I was a sponge around her. I spoke forty-three times that same year to my ideal clients.

My first speaking gig in September 2016 wasn't glamorous. It was in a quaint coffee shop, in a small Nevada town, with eight women. I didn't have any branding on my handouts and completely forgot to tell the women how they could work with me going forward. I certainly didn't knock it out of the ballpark. But I was good enough. To my surprise, I enrolled my first one-on-one high-ticket coaching client from that talk. I was dumbfounded and giddy. And the rest, they say, is history.

That simple, first speaking engagement was the most exciting day of my business. It was the day I started pursuing my dream. I remember thinking to myself, "Erin, enjoy this, and enjoy being new. Someday you will be expected to know what you are doing, and you don't want to miss the fun of speaking the first time and being bad." I have no idea where that thought came from. Maybe it's being the mother of three that kicked in and told me to enjoy all the firsts, because I knew I would never get them back.

That wisdom carried me so far that year. I enjoyed all the firsts. The first friend to join my email list. The first person to join my Facebook group. The first time I did a Facebook Live with hives all over my neck from anxiety. The first time I did a radio interview. The first time I interviewed on a podcast. The first time I wrote in a book compilation. I wanted to enjoy every step, because they were *mine*. My steps. My story. My fumbles. My victories.

The brain is wired for safety and order. It likes predictability and doesn't necessarily like new. As entrepreneurs, we need to tell our brains that we are going to fall in love with new. We need to tell our brains we are going to playfully experiment with trying things for the first time. And that starting small is a great, great thing.

Dr. Erin's Call to Action

1) Make a list of all of the firsts you have already been brave enough to experience in your business.

2) Now make a list of the firsts you have yet to experience, that you will welcome with playful curiosity.

3) Repeat after me: "I will fall in love with being new. I will be brave enough to start small. I will trust the right and perfect journey is unfolding for me."

Day 5
Balance Schmalance

"Success is liking yourself, liking what you do, and liking how you do it."

\- Maya Angelou

Balance is not achieved through equal time in all areas but through equal alignment in all areas.

Success is an inside job. It is individually defined and determined. What works for me may not work for you. So many times, people have come up to me and said, "Wow, Dr. Erin, you must be so busy." I hate the word "busy," and I know hate is a strong word. But busy and I broke up years ago. Who wants to be busy? Have you ever met a young child who says, "I want to grow up and be busy"? I have never met an adult who loves being busy. (Although I have met some who, unfortunately, wear it like a badge of honor.)

When people ask me, "How do you do it all?" I usually answer, "I don't cook or clean." That gets them curious. When I started this business in 2016, my husband Garth and I sat down and talked about what success looked like to us. It meant giving up the good for the great. It meant we weren't going to buy new furniture, but would instead keep the duct tape on the kitchen chairs for a while in order to invest any extra money in the business."

The same was true for our time. We knew I would be investing lots of time into the business, which meant I would have less time for other activities (like cooking and cleaning—*ha*). I haven't cooked or cleaned my house for over two years. Some would look at my life and say I was failing as a mother or wife. But here's the deal: what works for Garth and I would not work for all couples. My husband and I think we are winning.

I believe true success (and balance) is feeling aligned and fulfilled equally in all areas of your life. These areas include your family, love, work, relationships, physical health, spirituality, and finances. Instead of seeking equal time in all areas, seek equal levels of fulfillment in all areas. One person's definition of financial success will be different from another person's definition. This is how it is possible, then, for both you and I to report balance in our lives, even when you and I spend different amounts of time in each of the main areas of our lives.

Why is this so important? One of the greatest offenders to your success will be comparing. You comparing yourself to others and others comparing themselves to you. People will question how you spend your time and the price they believe you are paying for your success. If you are unclear about your personal definition of success, you risk missing your own target and hitting someone else's instead.

Pleasing others can easily take over and derail you completely. Your job is to please the people who are important to you, and no-one else. You are responsible to establish and maintain your own boundaries. Remember, what other people think of your boundaries is none of your business.

To some, my life would look like a completely imbalanced nightmare. To me, it's my dream life. It works for Garth, our children, and me. What works for you and your inner circle? If you don't define it, someone else will.

Dr. Erin's Call to Action

Rate your level of fulfillment in each of the major areas of your life. If one, or several, is out of alignment (perhaps below an 8), ask yourself how to adjust so that you are in full alignment.

Area of my life	**Rating—How Fulfilled Am**
	1 = not at all 10 = fully aligned
Family	_________________
Intimacy/Love	_________________
Work/Mission	_________________
Social Relationships	_________________
Physical Health	_________________
Spirituality	_________________
Finances	_________________

Day 6
The *Power* of ONE

"Our goal isn't to touch everyone, our goal is to touch someone. To change someone, just one person. If you get good at that, do five, then do one hundred. But stop worrying about everyone. Everyone doesn't matter."

-Seth Godin

Every day ask yourself, "How can I serve greatly today?"

I remember the first time I shared my big dream with another person. I couldn't believe I was going to vocalize this crazy, audacious, big, ridiculously silly, huge vision of mine. To this recovering perfectionist, such a thought in the past would have prevented me from even starting. Now I know it was part of the process of not only dreaming, but of turning my vision into a reality. I mustered up the strength. Would she laugh at me? Would she tell me to be realistic? Would she say, "Come on Erin, let's be practical."

I knew I needed just one moment of courage. It was time. I took a breath and said, "I have a vision for speaking in front of thousands of people. For changing the lives of thousands of people. They will come to my events. They will share me with their friends. All over the world." Writing the words here still gives me heart palpitations. Not from fear, but from excitement.

Why was it so hard to share my dream? Because I hadn't yet helped someone. I was just starting my speaking and coaching business. The thought of creating that vision, when I hadn't even created my first program or had my first live event, seemed so incredibly far away.

So, what was I to do? The same thing you are called to do. The same thing that every great mentor and leader of ours had to do. Start with the first step. Begin. Take the leap and go from there.

My first group coaching program required that first step. I hopped on the phone and invited the first person to join. My first Facebook group required that *one* step. I invited my first member. My email list required that *one* step. I shared my opt-in and added the first person. My first speaking engagement required that *one* step. I booked my first coffee shop and created my first presentation. My first high-end offer required that first step. I shared it, and the first person enrolled. And my first 1-Day Live event required that first step. I booked the coolest place in Reno, not knowing if anyone would come, and seventy-three people showed up. Then 150 came to the next event. I don't say this to impress you but to *impress upon you* the beauty that happens from choosing to start with *one* step.

In this age of digital marketing, tweets, likes, comments, and followers, we can lose sight of the fact that we are helping people. Real people. People aren't numbers. We live in a selfie culture, and we need to shift to a service model of reaching out to others.

Who can you help? Who is right in front of you that needs you to show up? Who is one person who needs the transformation you can provide? Start there. Help one person. Then help the next. Watch what happens when you do.

It's over two years since I shared that big crazy vision with my friend. As I look at my 2019 calendar, next month I speak a total of fourteen times all over the United States. I will inspire over 1,000 beautiful souls in January alone. I am taking my 1-Day Live event, Get Amped, on a North American tour in the United States and Canada. The vision is becoming a reality because I started with *one* step. You have to take the leap. It's required for your dream.

In the words of my mentor, Brendon Burchard, "You are stronger than you think. The future holds good things for you."

Dr. Erin's Call to Action

1) Brainstorm the business activities you have already accomplished that required you to start taking *one* step.

2) Now brainstorm the business activities in your future that will also require you to start at step *one*.

Day 7
Create
Affirmations That
Actually
Work

"Bliss is your birthright."
-Dr. Erin

I am grateful for all that I have and open to
receive all that I desire.

It was a hot, hot summer's day (I'm thinking about 103 degrees), and I was driving our free minivan that our friends had given us. Free often means *old*. Well, our minivan was so old it did not accurately register how much gas was in the tank. The minivan started sputtering and slowing down. We were running out of gas. I had our seven-year-old daughter, Emily, and our little one-year-old Zachary with me, and we were headed to meet friends at a swimming pool.

I started to vocalize my fear. "We are going to run out of gas in the sweltering heat." Emily sensed my worry and slight panic. In a harsh, firm tone, she stated abruptly, "Alright, people. We've got no room for negative thoughts. Only positive thoughts until we get to the swimming pool." When we pulled up to the pool and parked, Emily said with pride, "See, it works Mom."

Don't you wish it were that easy in our businesses? Don't you wish we could just think positively and everything we desired would come true? Don't you wish that when you have more month than money left over you could just say, "Alright, only positive thoughts from here" and the money would magically be deposited into your account?

By now you know that your self-talk can both radically change the course, and dictate the success or failure, of your business. You know you need to *mind your mind*. But did you know there is a right way and a wrong way to speak positively to yourself? How can that be?

Let me show you. Let's talk about positive affirmations. Psychological research says there is an ineffective way to use them. If not done properly, affirmations can increase shame, guilt, self-destructive thoughts, and self-hatred. Let me give you an example of how most of us have been taught to create and use affirmations.

Dana Carvey from *Saturday Night Live* showed us a comical but great example when he looked in front of the mirror and asserted, "You're good enough, you're smart enough, and doggone it, people *like* you." Maybe you've been told to think of your dream life and business and then assert to yourself that everything has happened. You proudly stand tall and say, "I am a millionaire." The problem with this is your brain knows differently. If you really are not a millionaire (yet), the unconscious brain will call you out on it as if to say, "Liar, liar, pants on fire." The brain knows the data, and it's hard to pull the wool over your brain's eyes.

We also greatly misuse affirmations when we confuse them with goals. Setting goals is necessary and extremely effective when growing a business, but when we use a goal for an affirmation, we enter dangerous territory. For example, if I set a goal to make $100,000 by the end of the year and then use that goal as an affirmation, I might say, "By the end of the year, I will make $100,000." The problem with using a goal as an affirmation is the psychological fallout if the goal is not reached.

Remember, the brain's job is to collect data, make sense of it, and then create order. The brain will attempt to protect us from feeling disappointment in the future. Time and time again, my clients have told me, "Dr. Erin, I'm afraid to use affirmations because I feel so bad when I don't reach my goals." They often say, "I'm scared to dream. I hesitate to create a vision for myself because if it doesn't happen, I'll feel foolish or ashamed."

We do not want to use our affirmations to pummel us. We want them to *affirm* us. So, how do we create affirmations that function effectively? Follow these five tips that science shows will supercharge the success of your positive thinking and help you manifest what you desire.

Five Tips for Creating Affirmations That Work

1) Start with something that is believable.

"I am open to receive money."

"I am open to receive my next five clients."

"I am committed to my goals/dreams and believe that my efforts will be rewarded."

2) Create affirmations in the present tense.

Instead of saying, "Someday" or "I will," say "I am _______," or "I am open to _______."

"I am creating long-term success."

"I am a person of action, and I am capable of holding a long-term view of my business."

3) Focus on what you want, not what you don't want.

Instead of saying, "I will remove debt," say "I am open to financial abundance."

4) Attach a state of positive feeling to your affirmations.

Generate some positive energy around your affirmations.

"I am so excited to be building my dream life."

"I am grateful for all that I have, and I work hard, and I am open to receive all that I desire."

"I am so glad I am capable of learning new strategies that can work for me."

"I enjoy learning how to _______."

5) Harness the power of intention.

"I intend to earn $5,000 every month, and I will work hard to achieve that number."

"I intend to increase my business by ten times this year."

Dr. Erin's Call to Action

Practice creating affirmations that really work. Follow the guidelines above and make your own below:

____

____

____

____

____

____

____

____

____

____

____

____

____

____

____

____

Day 8
Be like *Nike*

"*A little bit of greatness every day keeps mediocrity away.*"

-Dr. Erin

Feelings follow actions.

Nike had it right all along. Just do it. Most of the problems in our business can be solved with action. Behaviors. You know, the things that move the needle and create change and income.

So, why don't we *do it*? Why isn't it that simple? Why don't we write the blog when we have the idea? Why don't we call the prospect when we know we should? Why don't we follow-up with the person who said they were interested in learning more? Why don't we create our online program and share it with the world?

We *know* what to do, but we don't *do* what we know. It's called the Knowing-Doing Gap, and it is one of the biggest offenders in your business. The answer to "why" is simple but profound. *Our minds*. We think we need to wait for the *confidence* to do it. We will do it when we don't have the *fear*. We will do it when we can get it *perfect*. We will do it when we are *ready*. We will do it when we are *right*.

We've got it backwards. All backwards. We think that once we have the confidence, belief, motivation, and courage, then we will take action. But behavioral research shows that the opposite is true. It is in *doing* the action where our beliefs change.

Psychology 101: behave your way to better thinking, instead of trying to think your way to better behaving. I know, mind-blowing, right? It's hard, but it's effective.

For example, if you lack the confidence to be a public speaker, instead of trying to convince yourself you are a great speaker, you could hire a speaking coach, prepare, and then deliver your speech. In doing so, you will likely receive positive feedback from others, realize you did better than expected, and maybe even have some fun in the process. Your confidence will increase after you take action—even while being afraid.

How do you think your confidence will shift once you bumble your way through a sales call, and the prospect pays you? How do you think your belief in your product will increase once you launch it online and get your first ten paying customers? How do you think your motivation will improve once you get a testimonial from a client who says, "You changed my life"?

It's a simple philosophy but can be difficult to implement. Please understand all principles have promises behind them. And this one—to take action—works every time. If you need to, borrow my belief until you get your own. You've heard the saying, "The plan works if you work the plan." Work on this strategy, and I guarantee it will work. Research supports the idea.

Nike had it right. Confidence and motivation are highly overrated. Just do it. Close the Knowing-Doing Gap, and watch your business grow.

Dr. Erin's Call to Action

What actions do you need to do *right now* that will change the way you feel about yourself and your business?

Repeat after me: "I am a person of action."

Day 9

Break Up with *Your* Comfort *Zone*

"It takes courage to grow up and be who you really are."

-E. E. Cummings

[Outside my comfort is my zone.]

I remember it like it was yesterday. I was two weeks away from stepping on stage for a fitness competition. I had been training for ten months. Rigorous, brutal, transformational gym workouts and nutrition changes had completely changed my body, health, and mind.

D-day came. Monday, June 2, 2014. The day the competition suit arrived. All three inches of it. The itsy-bitsy-teeny-weenie-turquoise-rhinestone-string bikini was here. I tried it on and instantly started crying. I thought, "Jane Fonda called, and she wants her thong back." I thought I looked ridiculous. I knew I would never be ready to step on stage in two weeks. I would embarrass myself and feel ridiculous. I was devastated.

I went to the gym for my daily workout and started crying on the rowing machine. I told my trainer, Shelley, my fears. "I won't be ready in two weeks." She knelt down, looked straight in my eyes, and said, "Erin, can you work out, right now, for the next hour? What do you say?" I answered, through whimpers and tears, "Yes." Shelley then said, "Great. Can you eat what I tell you to eat today?" I took a deep breath and sighed, "Yessss." Then one last question, "Do you trust me?" I smiled, jumped up from the seat, and said, "I do. I trust you completely." Then she said something so profound, it has stuck with me ever since. These words have helped me countless times in my personal and professional life. She said, "Then borrow my belief until you get your own."

I decided right there in the weight room to trust her and reach for my goals. I did everything she told me to do. Two weeks later, I stepped on stage, at forty years old, and received a trophy in my first fitness competition.

And here's the thing. I stepped on stage with *fear*. Not with confidence. This experience was about as far out of my comfort zone as I could get. But I told myself, "Fear, come along. We've got a dream to chase. Here we go."

Two-time Olympic gold medalist David Wise attends our church here in Reno, Nevada. He told me when anyone asks him, "So, what do you do?" he answers, "I get uncomfortable as fast as I can." That's David's job description, and for high performers, it's also your job description.

Last year I was asked if I was interested in taking a leadership position in a women's business networking group. While I thought I would be great for the position, one of my trusted growth friends asked, "Dr. Erin, would you be *comfortable* doing it?" I answered quickly and emphatically, "*Absolutely*." To which he then replied, "That's exactly why you *shouldn't* take that position." Whoa. I learned an important lesson in that thought exercise.

Change and growth come from being outside our comfort zone. The faster you fall in love with fumbling and sometimes failing, the faster you will achieve your goals. Successful people fail often and fail fast. They fail faster than everyone else, and they get to the top faster than everyone else. It's called adopting a growth mindset.

To truly make it in business, I want you to grow your courage muscle. Really use it and strengthen it daily. Ask yourself often, "How can I stretch myself a little bit outside of my comfort zone?" When something seems a bit unfamiliar, new, challenging, or scary, run towards it. Know this is the path to your success.

I want you to climb what I call the Bad-Good-Great Ladder. Are you willing to be bad at something so that you can learn and improve? What are you so terrified to do in your business that it stops you from growing?

I want you to step out onto the skinny branches of the tree. You know, the scary place. This is where you will begin to experience real change and growth in your business. That's where the best fruit lies. I want you to be willing to start out bad, to become good, so that you can become great.

Dr. Erin's Call to Action

It's time for you and your comfort zone to break up. It's time to write your Dear John letter to your comfort zone. Follow this outline and say goodbye to comfort and hello to your new courageous self.

Letter to My Comfort Zone

Dear Comfort Zone,

It was love at first sight. We made a good pair.

At first, I thought you were good for me because:

____

____

____

____

But it's just not working out. I've changed and you haven't. It's time for us to go our separate ways. We have to break up because:

____

____

____

____

Love,
The new me.

Day 10
Invite Yourself to the *Party*

"You get in life what you have the courage to ask for."

\- Oprah Winfrey

Your success is a measure of your ability to receive.

Most successful people have a positive self-image. Some of that attitude comes from succeeding. However, it is impossible to begin moving toward success until you believe in yourself enough to go after your goals and dreams while learning to fail forward.

If you believe that you can't grow a profitable business, chances are you never will. As Henry Ford once said, "If you think you can or think you can't, you're right." The key to unlocking success in business and in life, lies in creating a strong self-image. How can you find this key?

I want to share with you one of my biggest little secrets to grow a successful business. This secret can radically change your business and improve your influence, income, and visibility. And here's the best news about this game-changing strategy…it's *free*.

- Want to know how I booked forty-three speaking gigs my first year in business? I asked.

- Want to know how I consistently get interviews on podcasts? I ask.

- Want to know how I sell-out my 1-Day Live events? I ask.

- Want to know how I spoke at a women's leadership conference with the most influential female leader in the area? I asked.

- Want to know how I went on 213 coffee dates in one year and exponentially increased my network? I asked.

- Want to know how I learned how to sell with ease? I asked.

- Want to know how I became a number one best-selling author on Amazon in six hours? I asked.

- Want to know how I was awarded Top 20 Most Powerful Women in Nevada? I asked.

- Want to know how I enrolled in my first online group course? I asked.

The strategy I have used more than any other is the power of the *ask*. I said this strategy is free, but there is actually a price you have to be willing to pay. You have to be willing to do the hard work. The *inside* work.

You have to be willing to invest in yourself until you believe you are worthy of receiving.

I want you to read that again.

Your *ability* to receive is a direct measurement of your *beliefs* about your worthiness of receiving.

I have spent countless hours in therapy, coaching, attending personal and professional development conferences, listening to podcasts, and reading hundreds of books in order to work on myself. But it's the kind of work that pays off in dividends.

The best investments you can make in your business are the ones you make in yourself. Your business will never outgrow you. Your business cannot outgrow your ability to receive. And your ability to receive is always limited by your beliefs about your worthiness.

Dr. Erin's Call to Action

Here are two ways to increase your self-esteem and thereby improve your chances of succeeding in the business world.

1) Be your own best fan.

Too often we are the opposite—we are our harshest critics by slamming ourselves in private for perceived errors in public. Those with high self-esteem and high self-efficacy are no less demanding of their performance, but they also support themselves with their own thinking and self-evaluation. They talk themselves up. They choose to interpret events in a positive way. They tell themselves that they can and will achieve.

Being your own cheerleader can take considerable self-discipline. But with consistent effort, we can become our most ardent supporters, rather than beating ourselves up inside. If we can pull it off, then inevitably our business performance will improve.

- Make a list of some recent accomplishments, successes, wins, and challenges you have successfully overcome. Write down your strengths. What do you like about yourself? When people compliment you, what do they say?

2) **Invest in your own competence.**

Generally, the more competent you are at business skills, the more confident you will be when doing them. Logical, of course. Yet so many entrepreneurs and executives are happy to coast on their previous studies and accumulated experience rather than dedicating themselves to ever higher levels of learning and competence in their fields.

When you think about it, it's clear that becoming highly competent has a dual reward. You get the benefits of that specific area of competence, but you also generally feel better about yourself. You feel more like a winner, which in turn leads to more confident actions/results.

Combine positive self-talk with ever-increasing task competence, and you have a powerful synergy of internal and external self-esteem boosters. It won't be long before what you think of yourself changes—and so will your entire future.

- Jot down some ideas of how you can invest in your personal and/or professional development. What skills can you learn, and where can you go to learn them?

Day 11
The 3 Cs of Confidence

"You are what you think you are."

-David Swarch

> Lack of self-discipline is not your problem.
> Alignment with your values is.

"I am 100% confident in every situation, 100% of the time," said no one ever. Confidence. It's something we all desire, and lack of confidence is something we have all struggled with at some point in our lives. As a psychologist and high-performance coach, I hear all too often how a lack of confidence prevents people from reaching their highest selves and achieving success in their business and personal lives.

I am so passionate about this topic because lack of confidence is a game changer. A deal breaker. It will take you out of the game if you don't recognize it and know how to manage it. Without confidence, your chances of being unstoppable disappear. So, what is confidence and how do we get more of it? Why do some seem to have gobs of it, and others struggle to find any at all? Is it something a person is born with, or can it be learned?

In my opinion, confidence is simply **the belief in one's ability to figure things out.** I want you to ask yourself, "Haven't I been through enough? What are some hard things in my life I have survived and handled?" I want you to realize you have a 100% success rate in surviving hard experiences and a great track record for figuring them out. You do. You really do. I'm confident about that statement.

Repeat after me, "Everything is figure-out-a-ble."

The keyword in my definition is belief. Our beliefs are the direct result of two things—the thoughts we think and the actions we take. The good news is that new research into neuroplasticity reveals that we can literally rewire our brains in ways that can positively change our thoughts and behaviors, at any age. What this means is it's never too late to become confident.

Thoughts and behaviors feed each other in a bidirectional way. In other words, you can think your way into different behaviors and behave your way into different thinking. Let me give you an example. Let's say you have a big speech to give, and you lack the confidence to present it well. What can you do? You can practice. Practicing and getting feedback from trusted people (the behavior) will change your thoughts ("I will present well because I have prepared"), leaving you feeling more confident about the upcoming speech. Presenting well will change your thoughts about your future ability to be a good presenter. This is called the competence-confidence loop. One of the best actions you can take to increase your confidence is to learn the skills necessary to do that behavior better and more skillfully.

As a psychologist, I think it needs to be said that sometimes confidence can be highly overrated. Sometimes, we are challenged to do things that are important to us, and we have little to no confidence in our abilities to do them. This is especially true for things we are trying for the first time. Our brains know the data and say to us, "You have no track record of success here. What do you think you're doing?"

In these situations, I would suggest two strategies that can be highly effective to grow one's confidence. The first is to **borrow the confidence of someone else,** and the second is to **grow your competencies** (i.e., your skillset).

One of my dreams was to host my own 1-Day event. I had very little confidence in my ability to know how to present to a group of close to one hundred people for eight hours! However, I knew that if I received the support and learned how to skillfully host my own events, I would be prepared, and my confidence would invariably grow. I knew of a coach in San Francisco who taught people like me to do exactly that, and I hired her! I knew she had a track record of hosting her own successful events and could teach me how. I borrowed her belief until I got my own.

Another way to build your confidence is to **keep the promises you make to yourself**. Think about a goal you have had that you did not meet. No self-judgment or shaming allowed here. First of all, I want to tell you, "It's not your fault." Why would I say that? Because what I know to be true about goal attainment is that it is more about our values than our self-discipline. Wanting something is very different than truly valuing it enough to take the actions to achieve it.

Show me what you spend your money on, and I will know what you value. Show me where you spend your time, and I will know what you value. Show me where you are most focused and organized, and I will show you what you value.

If you have not met a goal, it is most likely true that you truly didn't value that goal. You may have adopted the value system of someone else or chased a goal that really wasn't important to *YOU*. Smokers always find money for cigarettes. I always find money for coloring my hair, doing my nails, and self-development books and seminars (don't judge).

Confidence is a measure of your ability to confide in oneself. Keeping your word to yourself is the foundation that your confidence is built on. I didn't want to compete in a fitness competition because I wanted to be on stage in a tiny bikini. I competed because I wanted to stop eating Oreos. Let's be clear…I never wanted to stop eating Oreos. I wanted to stop being out of integrity with my value of being healthy and fit. I wanted to be in integrity so much that I was willing to say no to Oreos so that I could be true to my word and live a healthy lifestyle. It is really hard to like yourself, and hence confide in yourself, if you do not keep the promises you make to yourself.

Dr. Erin's Call to Action

Let's review the three ways to grow your confidence and what you can do to start today!

1) **Take personal inventory.** Make a list of the hard times you have survived and the challenges you have handled in your life. Realize you have the ability to figure things out. You can be confident right here, right now.

2) **Grow your skills/competencies.** What are three skills you can learn that will improve your success in your business in the next year? Who do you need to hire, or where can you learn these skills? Watch your confidence soar as your competencies grow.

3) **Keep your promises to yourself.** First, write down the top goal you have for your business in the next year.

   A) My big goal is: ________________________________

      Example: Making $500,000 this year, losing ten pounds, hiring a team.

      Now, write down the highest value you hold for yourself.

   B) What I value most is: ________________________________

      Example: Personal freedom, integrity, peace, joy.

      Now complete this sentence.

   C) How will (insert big goal from #1) making $500,000 fulfill my highest value of (insert highest value from #2) creating personal freedom?

*The answers to this third sentence, my friends, is your *why*. It is your reason for getting out of bed in the morning. It is what will keep you true to your word. It is what will replace willpower.

It is your higher purpose and your truest desire. When your *why* is strong enough, and clear enough, you can withstand any *how*.

> *"Go confidently in the direction of your dreams. Live the life you have imagined."*
> -Henry David Thoreau

Day 12
What Would My Ideal Self Do?

"Instead of asking, 'what do I want to be when I grow up?', let's ask ourselves, 'who do I want to be?'"

\- Dr. Erin

Be yourself, but be your best self.

Instead of asking, "What do I want?", what if we spent more time asking ourselves, *"who* do I value *being*?" Research shows we would feel alive, energetic, authentic, and present.

Successful people aren't different from you and me; they just activate themselves differently and more often. They set intentions regularly about who they want to be, the value they want to add to others, the feelings they want others to feel in their presence, and the energy they bring to situations. Do you know the question that Oprah began with at every single Harpo Studios staff meeting during her twenty-five years there? She always asked, "What is your intention for this meeting?"

Research shows that happy, engaged, confident, vibrant, energetic people have greater influence and make greater incomes. Successful people are happy, and happy people are successful. The surest way to be happy is to live your life in line with your values.

While I am a multi-passionate entrepreneur, I am also a multi-passionate woman. You are a multi-passionate person, too. In the coaching world, there is a concept called the wheel of life. It segments the various areas our lives, and the different roles we play, into six or sometimes seven areas. These most often include the following:

1) Mental

2) Spiritual

3) Financial

4) Work/Mission

5) Love/Family

6) Health

7) Social

What I want to suggest is we take a holistic approach to define and measure success. It *is* possible to be fulfilled and in congruence with our stated values in all areas of our life at the same time. Yep. You read that right. In fact, it's the working definition of high-performance. High performers succeed beyond standard norms, over the long-term, while having a sense of well-being and a healthy life full of positive emotions and relationships.

What gets me the most excited about being a high-performance business coach is the integrated approach I take. But there is one concept that is more important than all others. It drives the bus; it's the gas in the tank. It makes everything else flow. It's your *identity*. Who do you want to be?

How do you want to greet your family, lover, roommate, when you walk in the door after a long day at work? How do you want to show up to the meeting? What level of energy do you want to bring to the interactions with your children/employees/friends?

Purpose and meaning don't fall from the sky into our laps. We don't find them. They aren't lost. We listen and obey. We cultivate, behave, and create purposeful lives and businesses with intention.

Just like "the power plant doesn't have energy, it generates it" (Brendon Burchard), you don't need to find yourself. You need to activate yourself and ask who you want to be. Then you decide and behave accordingly. You choose and behave your way to your best self. And you reap the success of your best life.

Dr. Erin's Call to Action

Brainstorm all the words that would describe your best self. Your ideal self. If you were the person you desire to be, what words would describe that person?

Now choose your top three words from that list. Write them here.

1) ________________   2) ________________   3) ________________

Every day I want you to activate your best self/identity by reminding yourself of your three words. Some simple ways to do so include:

- Setting a timer on your phone every several hours to remind you of your three words.

- Writing your three words on a sticky note, and taping it to the bathroom mirror, or putting it on the dashboard of your car.

- Changing your wallpaper on your phone or your laptop screensaver to your three words.

- Tapping (look up EFT-Emotional Freedom Techniques). Tap your three words daily.

- Telling your accountability partners/growth friends, and reminding each other regularly.

Enjoy activating your best self in a consistent manner. Enjoy being intentional about who you want to be. Enjoy feeling fully alive and on purpose.

Lastly, I invite you to read this manifesto daily. It's my love note to my ideal self. I read this first thing every morning. It's my compass. It keeps me on course.

If you prefer, write your own manifesto. What do you take a stand for? What do you believe in? What would your most ideal self have you do, say, and be?

The AMPED Life Manifesto

I choose to live the amped life, the best life, the extraordinary life.

I am authentic, genuine, and have integrity.

The perfect and right people and opportunities present themselves to me.

I am not broken. There is nothing to fix. Bliss is my birthright.

I have massive value to bring and a lifetime supply of gifts to share with others.

Abundance is chasing me.

I am grateful for all that I have and open to receiving all that I desire.

I live with curiosity and adventure.

I am obsessed with greatness.

I am a person of action, and I move quickly.

I understand there is freedom in discipline.

I reach my goals with joy, ease, and confidence.

There is no failure when I learn. Because of this, I am in love with failing forward.

My life is unfolding perfectly.

I am activated, motivated, productive, energized, and disciplined.

I am courageous. I am brave. I am unstoppable.

Day 13
Stop Being So Funny About **Money**

"Money is the root of so much awesome."
- Dr. Erin

Bliss is your birthright.

A client of mine recently hired me because she had been building her business for four years and had not yet made any money. We tallied up the money she had spent on coaching, conferences, seminars, online courses, and personal development. She had spent over $100,000 on her business. When we explored her money mindset, she said, "I'm afraid my wanting money is a character defect, a bad fault of mine." She was worried she was greedy, ungrateful, and selfish. She would say things like:

"Dr. Erin, do I really deserve to make so much money?"

"Does it mean I'm greedy if I want more money?"

"People will think I am greedy if I make a lot of money."

"I must be selfish for wanting to make money."

Imagine poking your nose up to the glass that separates you from all the newborn babies lined up in the hospital nursery. Fresh and new, perfect, beautiful little babies. We would never walk up to one of them and say, "You deserve a good life, but only 50% of all the goodness." We would never limit the abundance that is waiting for any one of them. Yet, we do it to ourselves all the time.

I will boldly say that any thought you have told yourself that is *not* what you would say to those precious, newborn babies is just bad programming. Lies. Untruths you have learned from someone, somewhere, at some time. And the good news is…we can always rewire our brains.

I love in Jen Sincero's book *You Are a Badass at Making Money* when she says, "A healthy desire for wealth is not greed, it's a desire for life." She also has a great definition of 'rich', which she says is, "Being able to afford all the things and experiences required to fully experience your most authentic life." Who doesn't want to be rich?

If we cannot get over our fear of making money, we will never make any. Start by focusing on the value you are *giving* to others, not what you are *getting*. You *make* money; you don't *take* money. You offer value to those who deem it valuable; you don't push people to make choices they don't want to make.

I think of money as a medium of exchange. Money is a neutral conduit for a value exchange between two people. Person one says, "Hey. I've got this item. If you are looking for this item, it is this much money." Person two says, "Yes, I want that item (or I don't), and I am willing (or unwilling) to exchange this much of my money for it." It's a contract. An exchange of services rendered. Or value added. Or skills delivered. Or time saved. That's it.

The amount of the money you earn depends on your mindset of the value of your item and your beliefs about your worthiness to charge for the item. The amount of money you earn is not about the attitudes of your buyer or your worth on the planet. Your worth on the planet was established at birth. It's not up for discussion or based on someone's opinion.

Bliss is your birthright.

Dr. Erin's Call to Action

Take some time to answer these questions honestly. Would you agree or disagree with the following statements and beliefs about money?

- "Money is everywhere and is always available to me."

- "My bank account reflects the amount I am open to receive."

- "I can earn unlimited amounts of money by focusing on doing what I love."

- "When it comes to earning money, if it's easy, it's probably sleazy."
- "If you can cut a check for a problem, you don't have that problem."
- "It's OK to want to be rich!"
- "Money is the root of all evil."
- "Rich people are gross/greedy."
- "You can't be rich and spiritual."
- "Money isn't important."
- "Money can't buy happiness."
- "Money is out of my reach."
- "It's lonely at the top."
- "People who get excited by money are shallow."
- "Money ruins everything."
- "There will always be people who are willing to pay for my services."
- "Making money can be easy and fun."

Reflect on your answers. What beliefs are blocking you most from receiving more money? Write them here:

____

____

____

____

____

Let's create some new, healthy, vibrant money mantras to help you manifest abundance in your business and life. Choose any of the following or make your own.

Money Mantras/Affirmations

- I love money and money loves me.

- I'm grateful to money because _______________________.

- Money is neutral. It is a medium of exchange.

- Money is a blank slate that gets its value from the energy and meaning I give it.

- Money is the root of so much awesome.

- Every time I receive money, I will say to myself, "See, money loves me. It just can't stay away."

- I am grateful for all that I have and I am open to receiving all that I desire.

- Bliss is my birthright.

"If you don't make the money, you can't sustain the message."

- Brendon Burchard

Day 14
More *Self-Love* = More *Success*

Repeat after me. "Oh, how human of me."
- Dr. Erin

[**Stop 'should-ing' on yourself.**]

Hi, my name is Erin, and I am a recovering perfectionist. (This is where you say, "Hi, Erin.") For many, many years I masked my fear of not being good enough with performing, proving, and perfecting. I got the grades and degrees. I got the body. I won the awards. I excelled. I achieved. I tried to 'prove' my worth, and it nearly destroyed me. I was riddled with anxiety, a sense of never fitting in, and an extreme discomfort being in my own skin.

I look back on those painful years and realize I had what I call, a God-sized hole in my soul that I attempted to fill with worldly accomplishments, victories, and other self-destructive behaviors. Anything to make the pain go away. My lack of self-love eventually led to depression and a 'dark night of the soul'. I was emotionally bankrupt. My cup was empty.

It was during my emotional rock bottom that I found the gym. Yep, the gym. I decided to start taking care of myself. What started out as a physical transformation moved into a spiritual and emotional transformation. I started taking risks, being myself, sharing my true thoughts, and failing forward. I made mistakes, and I *loved* it. I had joined the human race. I finally felt like I belonged.

Through my weakness, I found strength. Through my vulnerability, I found power. Through my imperfection, I found beauty and strength. Instead of beating myself up when I made mistakes, I would say to myself, "Oh, how human of me."

The relationships that I had always wanted appeared in my life because I was learning to connect on an authentic and deep level. The financial success I had always desired started to appear as I worried less about making money and more about making an impact. I fell in love with stepping outside of my comfort zone, and in doing so, my perfectionism lost its oxygen supply. I learned that the best way to serve others is to first serve yourself. Not in a selfish way, but a self-*full* way.

One of my favorite thought leaders, Iyanla Vanzant, once said to Oprah, "How you treat yourself is how you treat God. Because *you* are the representative of God in your life. In your life, you've got to be as good to you as you want to be to God in order to be of service to others in the world."

Self-love truly is a win-win. It's not selfish to put yourself first. To be the best version of yourself is the most loving thing you can do—for yourself and for others. What comes out of the cup is for others, but what is in the cup is yours, and it's your job to keep your cup full.

"I fully and completely love, accept, and approve of myself." If you were to rate how true this statement is for you with 10 being, "Oh yes. This is exactly how I feel" and 1 being, "Haha. No way. I don't believe that at all", what number would you assign to yourself?

Psychological research shows that a person's level of self-worth is highly correlated with their level of success, happiness, and joy. The higher their self-worth, the higher their success, happiness, and joy.

As a psychologist treating clients for the past sixteen years, the common factor that all of my clients share is emotional pain. Psychologists and the majority of the great philosophers in the world would agree that the etiology—the cause—of that human suffering and pain stems from a lack of knowledge, and often a forgetting of one's worth. So, why does self-worth allude so many of us? Why do so many of us struggle with knowing our inherent worth and value?

I have good news and bad news. The good news is that bliss is our birthright. The bad news is that we often forget. We tend to 'should' on ourselves. We say things like:

"I should be farther along by now."

"I shouldn't have made that mistake."

"I should be better at sales."

"I should be making more money."

"I shouldn't have wasted all those years."

Let me share with you my top three strategies for increasing your self-love and, in turn, your success in business:

1) Behave your way into different thinking, instead of trying to think your way into different behavior.

Example: If you lack the confidence to be a great saleswoman, instead of trying to convince yourself you are great at sales, you could hire a sales coach, prepare, and then practice sales conversations with prospects. In doing so, you will likely receive positive feedback from others, realize that you did better than expected, and maybe even close some sales in the process. Your confidence will increase after you take action—even while being afraid.

2) Behave in ways that are consistent with your stated values.

Example: If being healthy and fit are goals and values of yours, but you treat yourself poorly by eating junk food and never exercising, it is going to be a tall order to feel great about yourself. But what if you treated your body as if you cared for it, feeding it nutritious foods and moving it regularly? You'd be behaving in line with your stated values. And when you do that, you have a much higher chance of liking yourself. It really is as simple, and profound, as that. So, keep those goals and values front and center in your mind. Remind yourself of them daily as they will continue to motivate you to 'act as if' you love yourself.

3) Start showing yourself compassion.

When was the last time you gave yourself credit for the life and business you are trying to create? When was the last time you documented, celebrated, or shared your wins? When was the last time you gave yourself grace and a pat on the back for taking risks in your business?

It is your time to rise from the ashes of self-doubt, low self-esteem and fear, and step into your greatness and personal power. And remember, when one person shines his or her light, it gives others permission to shine theirs. So shine on!

Dr. Erin's Call to Action

It's time to brag about yourself. To be proud. To celebrate. Spend some time documenting your success. Notice your wins. See your victories.

- What are you proud of?
- What have you accomplished so far?
- How have you been brave?
- How have you helped others?
- How have you stretched yourself?

Day 15
The
Wondering Technique

Instead of asking, "What if I don't succeed?", ask yourself, "I wonder how great it will feel when I do."

\- Dr. Erin

"Your curiosity is your growth point. Always." - Danielle LaPorte

If you want to grow your business, nothing is more essential than a large dose of curiosity. Psychologically speaking, curiosity is 360-degrees away from worry.

Worry sounds like this: "What if I don't reach my goals?" or "What if no-one signs up for my programs?" and "What if I no-one buys my product?"

Curiosity sounds like this:

"I wonder how great it will feel to enroll my next client."

"I wonder how beautiful the beach will be when I take my family to Hawaii."

"I wonder who I'll meet today at this networking event."

"I wonder how peaceful it will feel to see $20,000 in my bank account."

Neuroscience shows that our brain will find what we go looking for. What we focus on expands. If you are a woman who has ever been pregnant, you know what I mean. All of a sudden, all the pregnant people in the world come out of hiding. Or have you ever been car shopping, and suddenly the car you have your eyes on appears everywhere you look?

Cultivating Curiosity

So, how can we become 'seekers' and develop a curious attitude? The first thing to do is recognize the moments you feel uncomfortable. When you're avoiding a situation, it's a good sign that there's something novel there, something uncertain, and you can take advantage of that as an opportunity for growth.

Innovation, curiosity, and imagination are the secret brew that can take your career to the next level. These traits can also accelerate a company's profits and growth beyond its competitors. In a recent study, innovation was ranked a long-term challenge for driving business growth. It is a key talent needed at all levels of leadership, starting with the CEO.

Curiosity is a thirst for knowledge and the need to hunt for answers to these questions: "What is this?" and "How does it work?" It's an important mental exercise because it requires a mindset that helps people move forward and do new things that starts them on the path to new discoveries.

Curiosity is critical to your success because it's the strong desire to learn without constraint. It's the driving force behind new discoveries in all fields.

Here are three reasons why curiosity is critical to your success:

1) **There is a link between intelligence, emotion, and curiosity.**

In a recent *Harvard Business Review* article, Dr. Tomas Chamorro-Premuzic, a professor of business psychology at University College London, identified three qualities that are essential if we are to successfully manage the complexity of modern life. The first two are intellectual acuity and emotional intelligence.

Complex environments are dense with information, which requires more brainpower or deliberate thinking. Our IQ is a measure of that brainpower, just like megabytes are a measure of a computer's capacity. High IQ levels enable people to identify and solve more problems. Intelligence is a strong predictor of performance on complex tasks. Studies now show, however, that using our smarts is not enough to ensure success.

Soft, interpersonal skills are also essential if we want buy-in from others. Emotional intelligence is an important component of mental toughness because we need to manage our emotions, thoughts, and behavior in ways that will set us up for success.

People who are socially savvy are better equipped to navigate organizational politics and advance their careers. Most employers look to people with good emotional intelligence and soft skills when it comes to management and leadership positions.

Curiosity is the third quality that Dr. Chamorro-Premuzic believes is as important as intellect and emotional savvy. Curiosity is critical to your success because it signals a hungry mind. If you're inquisitive, you're open to new experiences. You can generate more original ideas and produce simple solutions to complex problems.

2) Curiosity makes you a more interesting person.

Curiosity is critical to your success because when you are curious, something interesting happens — you come across as more interesting and more intelligent. Others will interpret your curiosity as intelligence.

Curious people have active minds. The mind is like a muscle that becomes stronger through continual exercise; curiosity is a mental exercise that makes our minds stronger. Studies show that people are better at learning information when they are curious about the topic.

In his 1994 paper, *The Psychology of Curiosity*, George Loewenstein found that curiosity requires some amount of initial knowledge. His research determined that we are not curious about those things we know absolutely nothing about. This changes, however, when we start to learn even a little bit about a topic or subject; our curiosity is piqued, and we want to learn more. It turns out that the more we know, the more we want to know.

3) Curiosity sends the right message.

As a leader, entrepreneur, or small business owner, the need to send the right message is constant. It's important to convey the message that you prefer to ask the right questions rather than pretend to know all the answers. Too often, this becomes

flip-flopped when the emphasis is to know all the answers —
a sure path to stagnation.

Curiosity is important to every business owner, entrepreneur, and leader. If it wasn't, new ventures would have no appeal. When we ask questions and maintain a strong sense of curiosity, we see a person for who they truly are and a company or market trend for what it truly is.

Dr. Erin's Call to Action

I want you to practice being curious. **Be interested, not interesting.**

Apply the wondering technique to your life and your business. Make a list below of ten wondering statements. Remember, this is a very powerful technique, so only wonder about the things you truly desire will happen.

Ready…set…grow.

1) I wonder…

2) I wonder…

3) I wonder…

4) I wonder…

5) I wonder…

6) I wonder…

7) I wonder…

8) I wonder…

9) I wonder…

10) I wonder…

Day 16
Behave Your Way *to* Success

"We are what we repeatedly do. Excellence, then, is not an act, but a habit."

-Aristotle

> A little excellence every day keeps mediocrity away.

Research by my mentor Brendon Burchard shows that high performers consistently engage in six specific habits. He studied hundreds of high performers—people who create ever-increasing levels of both well-being and external success over the long-term—and found they have six habits in common. You can read about them in his best-selling book, *High Performance Habits*.

Let me share how I have consistently practiced these six habits in my business. Then, I challenge you to start using them in yours.

1) Seek clarity.

> **Me**: With my coaching clients, I always start with the same question: "So, tell me what you want, what you really, really want?" (cue *Spice Girls* singing). This year my goal was to meet Brendon Burchard and enroll in his coaching programs, and I did both.

> **You:** I want you to have laser focus for the next year on your business goals. How many clients do you want to serve? What income do you want to make? How many speaking engagements do you want to secure? How much do you want to grow your email list?

> Whatever your goals are, get super-duper specific and focused. It will make you insanely productive, happy, and will help you say "yes" and "no" to the right things.

2) Generate energy.

> **Me:** People always ask me, "Dr. Erin, how do you have so much energy?" I will tell you—I generate it. I am intentional about the energy I bring to a room, to my family, to my workouts, to a coffee date, and to my business meetings. Energy isn't something that just some people have. Energy is a choice. I also take care of myself physically. I take breaks

throughout the day, pray, meditate, journal, exercise, and eat well. All these self-care activities *give* me energy rather than take away energy.

You: The next time you head into a meeting or walk into your house at the end of a day, rate your energy on a scale of 0-10. Try to raise it by 1-2 points, right then and there.

3) Raise necessity.

Me: I knew when I started my coaching business I had to learn how to sell and fall in love with selling. It was crucial for my mission because my business depended on me making money, and my mission depended on my business being successful. I hired two sales coaches, and within one year won the honor of Nevada's Professional Saleswoman of the Year.

You: Instead of pushing yourself, ask, "What lights me up so much that when I do it, it *pulls* me?" It's almost like you just *have* to do that thing because it is either 1) your purpose here, 2) you feel called, or 3) it brings you so much joy.

4) Increase productivity.

Me: I appear insanely productive because I'm insanely clear about what I want and have become really good at setting and keeping boundaries. If it doesn't further my dream, I don't do it. Productivity is a function of how well you are leading your dream.

You: Don't go to work without your dream in the front of your mind. Break up with busy. Be intentional about your time. Ask yourself, "Does this further my dream?"

5) Develop influence.

Me: John Maxwell, the great leadership guru, says leadership is a function of influence, and the only way to have influence is through connection. In my first year of business, I went on 213 coffee dates. I am now reaping the rewards of influence as a result of connecting with enough people and asking them two questions: 1) Tell me about you, and 2) What do you need/how can I help?

You: High-performance is social. You are not supposed to do this alone. Connection is a sure way to grow your confidence as well. The person who serves the most will be the most successful, so how can you get busy serving others in your business? When you help enough people get what they want, you have a really good chance of getting what you want.

6) Demonstrate courage.

Me: Oh boy, this is a biggie. I have stretched myself in so many areas this year. I have raised my rates when I was scared it would turn people away (nope). I have booked speaking engagements with groups of people that intimidated me (I'm speaking to a huge social media agency in San Francisco next month as a result of that one). I decided to take my AMPED 1-Day Live event on tour across North America in 2019. I started a podcast and charged people for being on it (don't see anyone else doing that). I quit things that no longer served me, even though I feared people would question my character.

You: Remember, your job is to get comfortable being uncomfortable. If you aren't uncomfortable, you aren't dreaming big enough. If you reach every goal you set for yourself, you aren't dreaming big enough. If you don't get butterflies in your stomach on a regular basis, you aren't dreaming big enough. The magic happens out on the skinny branches of the tree. Get out there and watch what happens.

You've got this. You deserve the high-performance life.

Dr. Erin's Call to Action

Take some time to assess your level of achievement and alignment in each of the six success habits. If you score below a 10, ask yourself what 1-3 actions you can take to increase your score.

Non-existent   I am awesome

1) Clarity   1   2   3   4   5   6   7   8   9   10

     1-3 actions I can take to improve my clarity:

2) Energy   1   2   3   4   5   6   7   8   9   10

     1-3 actions I can take to improve my energy:

3) Necessity   1   2   3   4   5   6   7   8   9   10

     1-3 actions I can take to improve my necessity:

4) Productivity   1   2   3   4   5   6   7   8   9   10

     1-3 actions I can take to improve my productivity:

5) Influence   1   2   3   4   5   6   7   8   9   10

1-3 actions I can take to improve my influence:

6) Courage   1   2   3   4   5   6   7   8   9   10

1-3 actions I can take to improve my courage:

Day 17
Find Something *Sexy* About *Sales*

"Find a problem, then solve it."
-Dr. Erin

"I'm just looking for people who are looking for me."

"I *love* sales," said no psychologist ever. I didn't start my own business for six years because I didn't see myself as a saleswoman. "I'm a psychologist, I help people, I don't sell things," I would tell myself, as if they were mutually exclusive categories. I knew I needed to get over my fear of sales if I wanted to make an impact, serve people, and build a profitable business. So, I hired a sales coach, and she confirmed what I already knew…

I was *terrible* at sales.

However, what I lacked in skills I made up for in earnest effort. I was on a mission to *learn* how to get great at sales. I practiced and practiced and practiced. And I did what I knew best—I connected and served people.

During those 213 coffee dates I mentioned earlier, I got to know people. Really *know* them. I listened way more than I talked. I tried to figure out what they wanted and needed. And then I got busy serving them—helping in any way I could.

My influence grew, and my visibility grew too. People started to know, like, and trust me. I started to fall in love with selling—because I fell in love with serving.

As a psychologist, I realized I was naturally equipped to be awesome at sales. After all, I am trained in:

1) Listening

2) Asking great questions

3) Discovering what problems need solving

I then realized:

Sales = Finding and then fixing a problem. To me, this is the essence of sales.

And the good news is that the skills I have as a psychologist are the same ones that you either 1) already possess, or 2) can quickly learn.

I want you to think of Santa Claus. Santa cannot possibly pull out the perfect gift for *you* until he knows what is on *your* wish list. If you can get great at figuring out what your ideal client wants, you will never have to convince anyone to do anything ever again.

It's that's simple, and it's that fun.

Dr. Erin's Call to Action

Follow this four-step sales conversation script and watch your sales soar, I call it, Mind the Gap. It is your job to help your client identify their gap—the gap is that space between where they currently are and where they want to be.

These are the same four steps I take in the sales conversations I use, teach my coaching clients to use, to enroll ideal clients and grow our impact, income, and influence.

1) **Identify the gap.**

    What are you trying to accomplish this year?

    What do you think you would need to double your business (or happiness) this year?

2) **Widen the gap.**

    What strategies have you already tried to improve your business (or life) that worked and didn't work?

    The answer to this question is marketing gold. Use it in your sales pages and email copy.

3) **Bridge the gap.**

    First, summarize what you heard the client say, reflecting back what you heard. For example, you can say, "So, if I were to summarize what I heard you say, it would be…" or "What I heard you say is…"

Second, really validate how hard they have been trying to figure out how to solve their problems.

Third, recognize and acknowledge their perseverance and being a person who is seeking help and support.

Fourth, ask, "What would it mean to you to finally remove these obstacles and reach your goal?" (This is where you start to bridge the gap.)

4) Close the gap.

Say these exact words: "I can help with that, I've got a suggestion. Would it be okay if I shared it with you?" Then proceed to tell them all the ways you help people solve the exact problems they just told you they have.

Happy serving and happy selling.

Day 18
Move from
Probability to Possibility

"I'm not interested in what is probable. I'm interested in what is possible."

-Dr. Erin

The power of the pivot.

As a business owner or entrepreneur, you constantly need to take your skillset and mindset to the next level. You are reaching levels you have never seen or experienced before. Knowing how the brain works, and how it can sometimes feel like it is sabotaging those efforts, will make all the difference in your success.

I just got off a coaching call with my business coach, and my 2019 goal is to increase my income ten times. That would mean this is the year I become a millionaire. Guess what thought my brain immediately sent me? "Good *Lord*, Erin. That's impossible. You've never even come close to making a million dollars." Can you relate to my thought?

So, why does the brain do this? Why does it seem to thwart our efforts to reach new levels of success? Knowing why brains do this, and what to do about it, is paramount in your ability to 1) notice it, and 2) change it to work in your favor. Let's talk about brains, baby.

Brains do what brains do. Their job description is to collect data, assimilate it, make sense of it, and provide algorithms (rules and guidelines, so to speak) so you can make sense of your world and feel safe and in control. Again, it's really helpful—until it's not.

Let's compare this to the job of an entrepreneur and business owner. Your job is to try new things, take risks, stretch yourself, and be courageous. Yikes, that's a tricky combination. You can see that if you don't train your brain to think a certain way about your business, it can easily take you out of the game!

If I were to have the thought I shared above, and then fully believe it as truth, I would agree with that thought and not push myself to do the activities in my business that would help me create a million dollars. Fear would win, and my potential success (and dream of being a millionaire) would lose.

So, this is the shift we need to make. We need to train our brains to move from their default programming—which is all about **probability** (what has happened in the past. What is likely to happen in the future given the data collected so far?)—and move into the land of **possibility** (have other people become millionaires? Can I learn how to generate a million dollars? Can I create new strategies to create new revenue streams? Even though I have never earned a million dollars, is it possible for me?).

Once we have a non-judgmental stance of our thinking, we can observe the thoughts our brains send to us and then *choose* what we want to do with them. I call it **the power of the pivot**. We can learn how to observe our thoughts and then choose how we want to react to them. Exciting, I know.

The next time you notice yourself experiencing some stinkin' thinkin', it is highly likely your brain is just doing what brains do naturally. It is your opportunity to practice the power of the pivot.

I have created a four-step strategy that will help you manage any negative thought that should involuntarily invite itself to the party. I call it, **Bless and Release.**

Let's walk through it together below.

Dr. Erin's Call to Action

Four-Step Bless and Release Method

1) **Observe and validate your thought.**

   Example: My stinkin' thinkin' tells me, "Erin, you are crazy to think you can be a millionaire."

   What's your thought? Write it here. _______________________.

   Now, complete this sentence:

"It makes perfect sense you showed up right now because
___________________________."

I could say, "It makes perfect sense you are showing up because you work from data. You are correct, I have never been a millionaire before."

2) **Say "Thank you" to your thought.**

I know, sounds crazy. Remember, your brain is there to try to create order, protect you, keep you safe, and in control.

Example: "Thank you for trying to keep me safe as I consider going after a huge, crazy goal."

3) **Tell your thought you no longer need it**

Tell your thought that the rules have changed. Maybe you are safe now in ways you weren't in the past. Maybe you have skills or a support system you didn't have in the past. Whatever the case, you need to tell your brain that things are different now, and you are capable of change.

Example:

"Thank you for helping me in the past and protecting me."

"Thanks for trying to keep me safe, but I no longer need you. I am safe now without you."

"Thanks for trying to make me feel in control, but I need to take some educated risks to reach new levels of success."

What do you need to tell your thought? ___________________

4) **Pivot.**

Now it is time to tell your brain what you are going to do. Tell your brain the choice you are now going to make, and the actions you are now going to take.

Example: "I now choose to use my new strategies to earn my first million dollars."

What do you need to tell your brain? ___________________________

Congratulations. You now have the psychological tool to non-judgmentally observe your thoughts and challenge them when they do not serve you. There is so much freedom in this technique. It truly is life-changing when *you* start telling your brain what to think, rather than your brain telling you how to think.

Day 19
Assemble Your Personal Board of *Directors*

"You are the average of the five people you spend the most time with."
-Jim Rohn

In my head, Oprah and I hang out all the time.

A large part of my business model is focused on interpersonal relationships. High-performance is social. Humans are social creatures, and we constantly engage in relationships with others through work, school, social media, and elsewhere. Human connection is an important part of our lives, and we make a point to interact with the people we feel closest to. Our relationships have a huge impact on our well-being and, therefore, on the success of our businesses.

Want to be successful? Surround yourself with successful people.

Want to be happy? Surround yourself with happy people.

Want to be healthy? Surround yourself with healthy people.

Want to become more confident? Surround yourself with confident people.

In essence, we become more like the people we hang out with.

Take a moment to reflect on the following: Who are the people you spend the most time with? Do they elevate you or bring you down? Are they proactive go-getters exhibiting qualities that you admire or people who just sit and criticize? Do they motivate or drain you?

The awesome benefit about being around positive-minded individuals, who have a habit of chasing their dreams and believe in taking responsibility for their lives, is that you'll be inclined to grow in a positive direction as well. They will have an impact on your thinking and consequently your behavior. They will support you on your journey and move you towards inspired action. Maximize the amount of time you spend with these people!

"Associate only with positive, focused people who you can learn from and who will not drain your valuable energy with uninspiring attitudes. By developing relationships with those committed to constant improvement and the pursuit of the best that life has to offer, you will have plenty of company on your path to the top of whatever mountain you seek to climb."

-Robin Sharma, Leadership Expert

As I said previously, I call these people your **growth friends**. They are different from 'maintenance' friends. You know, the people you might watch the Super Bowl with once a year, or chit-chat with at the kid's soccer game. It's great to have a lot of friends. However, the key is to have the proper social interactions and the proper interpersonal relationships to achieve success and happiness in your life. Not everyone is going to be in support of your success and your dreams. Who are you going to let into your circle?

Dr. Erin's Call to Action

Make a list of the people you interact with on a monthly basis (continuously). This doesn't include the woman at the checkout counter at the local grocery store—really think. Narrow that list down to the five people you interact with the most. Don't create judgments around these people just yet. This should be a true list of who is within your current circle, the people who you essentially have the closest relationships with.

Now ask yourself the following questions for each of the five people who made your list.

1) **Does this person want the best for me?** This is a simple question but an important one. Does this person want what I want in terms of my success journey?

2) **Do their values align with my values?** This will eliminate a majority of people. This should go beyond your core values. What do you value in terms of your income, health, and inner-self?

3) **Do they increase my energy levels?** This is self-explanatory, but a difficult question to answer. There are some people within our lives who bring us down. Sometimes, we unintentionally surround ourselves with negative people or people who don't want to see us be successful.

4) **Am I willing to invest effort and time into this relationship?** I will say it over and over again: protect your time. It is the one thing we cannot control. Interpersonal relationships take effort and time to maintain. Is this person worth your time?

5) **Can I provide value to this person?** This is the most important question. Your circle of influence should not just be about you and what you bring to the table. A relationship is effective because that person is filling a need, and, in turn, you are filling a need for that person as well. Relationships are a two-way street.

Evaluation

Ideally, you should be able to answer "yes" to all five questions. Circle the names of the people who have a yes for each question. Do not focus on getting five people within your circle of influence. Be honest. If you only have one, that's OK. I've seen so many entrepreneurs struggle with creating positive interpersonal relationships. It is important to understand that leaving people outside of your circle of influence is fine.

I need to point out here the difference between *judgment* and *discernment*. I am not asking you to judge another person's worth. I am not asking you to judge whether they are a good person or a bad person. What I am asking you to do is to use the tool of discernment. I am asking you to discern whether spending time with that person is a positive decision for you. How does being in a relationship with that person work for you? Your circle of influence should be composed of people who care about your goals and can be helpful in your times of need.

What if you don't have five people? Remember, that's OK. You can find them in books, on podcasts, etc. Assemble your own personal board of directors. If you could choose anyone to sit on your board, who would you choose? Oprah would be on mine, along with Brendon Burchard, Jesus, my husband, and some other people. Imagine consulting your personal board of directors when you face difficult decisions? What would Jesus do? How would Oprah handle this problem? How would Brendon advise me if I shared my struggle with him?

The amazing advantage about where we are today, in terms of technology, means that you can literally surround yourself with inspiring people (e.g., through Twitter, Facebook, podcasts, audiobooks). As a result, I've put together a few ideas including these more modern methods on how you can begin creating a more optimal environment for your personal growth and success:

- Attend events in your local town/city that appeal to your interests, can help you learn something useful, or arouse your curiosity. Make sure to bring your business cards with you.

- Seek out people who have skills/qualities that you admire and learn from them. Never assume that they have nothing to learn from you. We can always learn something from someone, regardless of where they are in their own life.

- Minimize the time you spend hanging out with the wrong crowd and unhealthy influences, (e.g., pessimists and those that can hurt your chances of achieving success).

- Read more. Books, blogs, etc. You will be exposed to inspiring success stories, expand your library of knowledge, and nurture your creative thinking.

- Listen to audiobooks/podcasts when you are commuting and/or relaxing.

- Follow inspirational people that you can learn from on social media.

- Subscribe to newsletters, which will add value to your life and help you towards your goals in life.

- Keep perspective. It's important to spend your time with those who are more successful than you. It is also great for your development to be around those who are at the same stage as you (so ideas and the journey can be shared) and those below you, who you can inspire and share your wisdom with.

- Spend less time in front of the TV and your smartphone, and more time getting out there and connecting with people. You just never know where those connections will lead.

Day 20
Claim Your Expert *Status*

"What if Beyoncé had said, 'Does the world really need another singer?'"

-Dr. Erin

The world needs you to be *you*. #BeLikeBeyoncé

Again, I hear it time and time again as a business coach. Fear of not being credible. Fear of not being qualified. Fear of not being an expert. It shows up in various ways and sounds like this:

Who am I to be a coach?

Who am I to help people with this?

Who am I to (insert dream)?

Aren't there already so many (insert job title) in the world?

What makes me any different?

Am I credible enough to do this work?

What makes me better than all the rest?

Is there really room for me?

Does the world really need me?

I could never be like so and so.

Will anyone even take me seriously?

I don't have a Ph.D. like you, Dr. Erin. I don't even have a degree.

Can you relate? I thought so.

Even I wasn't immune from this kind of thinking popping up in the early stages of my coaching career. I remember asking my coach, "How can I just say I am a business coach? I've never been a coach before, and I've never owned my own business before." She then lovingly reminded me I had been a successful psychologist in my own private practice for fifteen years and had a great track record of helping people change their mindset and lives.

And then it hit me. My credibility wasn't about me. My credibility was about the change I could make happen for my clients. It was about the transformation I could help my clients achieve. It was about the problems I could help my clients solve.

Credibility is not about you, your past, or your credentials. **It is about the value you can add to others**. Your credibility resides in your ability to offer a new perspective to your clients. Your credibility, and therefore what you get paid for, is your ability to help others go from where they are to where they want to be—faster than they could do it without your assistance.

I think this is such great news. You are uniquely credible. And you are also uniquely an expert. By definition, an expert is "anybody who can inspire and instruct others how to improve their lives and achieve their goals."

You are alive at a time when there has never been more opportunity to grow a successful business. You can teach any topic to anyone you decide, whenever you decide to start, and have an incredibly lucrative career doing it. In the next two years alone, more than 40% of the global population will have access to high-speed internet.

It's time to claim—and be paid for—your status as an expert.

Dr. Erin's Call to Action

1) Make a list of all the **problems** your ideal client has. What do they want to be solved? What obstacles or difficulties do they want to be removed? What problem could someone help them solve, and they would happily hand over their credit card to get it done?

2) Make a list of your ideal client's **aspirations**. What do they want? What do they long for? What do they dream about?

These problems and aspirations are both areas where you can claim your expert status. As Jerry Maguire said, "Help me help you." Credibility and expert status is about them, not you.

<u>Problems</u>   **<u>Aspirations</u>**

______________________   ______________________

______________________   ______________________

______________________   ______________________

______________________   ______________________

______________________   ______________________

______________________   ______________________

______________________   ______________________

______________________   ______________________

______________________   ______________________

______________________   ______________________

______________________   ______________________

______________________   ______________________

______________________   ______________________

______________________   ______________________

Day 21
Find Your
Garth

"Choose a job you love, and you will never have to work a day in your life."

-Confucius

["Be obsessed or be average." - Grant Cardone]

I was in graduate school in a research team meeting with our advisor and faculty member, Dr. O'Donohue. He was helping each of us decide what we would choose as our dissertation topic. We would spend countless hours and several years of our lives dedicated to the subjects we chose, so we had better like the topic. Dr. O'Donohue knew Garth and knew my love for him—we had been dating for five years. He really liked Garth and knew I was head over heels for him.

That afternoon Dr. O'Donohue compared finding your research topic to dating. He said, "Sometimes you have to explore different research topics before you find the one you really enjoy. It's kind of like dating. Sometimes you have to kiss a few frogs before you find your true love." But he was adamant about one thing—it was really important to research something you were passionate about, cared about, would enjoy exploring, and was exciting enough to spend your career being known as an expert in that area. I've never forgotten what he said next. "When it comes to research, you need to find your Garth."

Every day, for as long as I can remember, I have told our two girls, Grace and Emily, "Find your Garth." It's not that I think women need a man to be whole or complete, and I certainly don't believe us women can't be self-sufficient. It's my funny way of honoring how awesome I think Garth is. I like to joke, "I got ninety-nine problems, but Garth ain't one of them." I don't have that many problems because I "found my Garth," but it's funny to say. He is the best thing that has ever happened to me.

When it comes to building your business, I implore you to find your Garth. Find what sets your soul on fire. Find what gives you energy and makes you better as a result of doing it. Find what gives you joy. Find what makes you smile and laugh. Find what feels so fun you cannot believe you get paid to do it.

Don't stop until you find that joy. High performers don't use words like "grind" and "hustle." High performers are happy and successful because they feel called to do their work, out of a joy-filled necessity. They wake up and joyfully live their mission. Instead of proving and pushing and trying to *make* things happen, high performers feel *pulled* by their calling, and it creates a sense of ease and flow.

As you continue to grow yourself, your business, and your dreams, I leave you with this:

"A master in the art of living draws no sharp distinction between her work and her play; her labor and her leisure; her mind and her body; her education and her recreation. She hardly knows which is which. She simply pursues her vision of excellence through whatever she is doing and leaves others to determine whether she is working or playing. To herself, she always appears to be doing both."

-Lawrence Pearsall Jacks, Educator, and Philosopher

My greatest wish for you is to find your Garth. You are so deserving.

God bless you,

Dr. Erin Oksol.

What's Next?

Let's go on safari. One of my dreams is to go on an African safari. How about you? I can just imagine the scenery, the wide-open spaces, the still in the air, the majestic sunsets, and the magnificent lions and giraffes.

Okay, we aren't going on safari—at least not yet. But when I do, what I know for sure is I will hire a tour guide. Someone who knows the route and the best views. The dangers and how to avoid them. Someone who'll make sure I won't be eaten alive.

Coaching is like that scenario. When starting or building a business, it's important to have a guide. Building a business on your own can be scary. (*Lions, and tigers, and bears, oh my.*) I know the feeling. You want someone who's been there, done that and got the T-shirt. Someone who knows the mistakes to avoid. How to get you to your destination faster and with less frustration, overwhelm, and setbacks.

Let me be your tour guide in business. Let me help you navigate unknown territory so you can enjoy the journey with less fear.

It's time to **stop**:

- Spinning your wheels.
- Having lots of great ideas but no clue how to package them into an offer that sells.
- Feeling overworked and underpaid.
- Feeling scattered and overwhelmed.
- Feeling exhausted, stressed, and fatigued.
- Spending more money on your business than you make.

It's time to **start:**

- Feeling joy, confidence, and ease around your work.

- Attracting your ideal clients with ease.

- Experiencing crystal-clear clarity and vision.

- Falling in love with selling.

- Replacing burnout and exhaustion for ease and vitality.

- Bringing balance back to your life.

- Making the money and impact you desire.

I want to invite you to join my advanced training programs and community of high performers. We're here to help you create a profitable business and experience joy, happiness, and great success.

Please visit my website **www.thepsychologyofmission.com** to learn more. It would be my honor to serve you.

Parting Words of Wisdom

I pray this book has felt like a roadmap for successfully navigating the sometimes-dangerous territory of your brain. You are not alone on this journey and have twenty-one new tools you can pull out of your business tool-belt when needed.

Here's what I know:

- Somedays you just need to tell the itty-bitty-stinkin'- committee inside your head to shut up.

- The brain can be a dangerous neighborhood. Or it can be your BFF and best business partner.

- You are the one who talks to yourself the most. Tell your brain a good story.

- You were not born with your *current* brain. You can train it to think differently.

- Doing things alone is so 1982. High-performance is social. Find your tribe and get support.

- Think of a good business coach as a tour guide. Been there, done that. Bought the T-shirt.

- In order to grow your business, you need to find something sexy about selling.

- Fall in love with starting. Fall in love with being new. Fall in love with learning. Fall in love with not knowing.

- If you reach all your goals, you are not dreaming big enough.

- Entrepreneurship ain't for sissies, but it's tons of fun.

- Your brain is like a computer. Hit 'delete' if it sends you a crappy thought.

- Bliss is your birthright.

- It's time to step into your greatness.

- You have enough. You do enough. You *are* enough.

- Time is an illusion. You are not behind. Your life is unfolding perfectly.

- Your light may be too bright for some. Keep shining.

- You are an *epic* human being.

You are unstoppable.

About Dr. Erin

Dr. Erin Oksol is a high-performance business coach, psychologist, professional speaker, and four-time best-selling author. She is the founder of Success with Dr. Erin Coaching and Consulting. Her mission is helping business owners/ entrepreneurs turn their passions into profits, creating massive impact doing what they love. She was recently named one of the Top 20 Most Powerful Women in Nevada and earned the award of Saleswoman of The Year by the Professional Saleswomen of Nevada.

With fifteen years and over 15,000 hours of clinical experience as a psychologist and coach, Dr. Erin brings her expertise in human behavior and change to help others go from where they are to where they want to be, so they can create a business and life they are obsessed with. She is married to Garth and has three children: Grace, Emily, and Zachary.